FROGS

by Peter Murray

The Child's World®

Content Adviser:
Winston Card,
Conservation Program
Manager, Cincinnati Zoo
& Botanical Garden

Published in the United States of America by The Child's World®
PO Box 326 • Chanhassen, MN 55317-0326
800-599-READ • www.childsworld.com

PHOTO CREDITS
© Dante Fenolio/Photo Researchers, Inc.: 27
© David Trood/Getty: 28
© Fritz Rauschenbach/zefa/Corbis: 21
© George Grall/Getty: 13 (bottom)
© Joe McDonald: 7, 18–19
© Joe McDonald/Corbis: 25
© John Tinning; Frank Lane Picture Agency/Corbis: 13 (top)
© Mark Moffett/Minden Pictures: 11
© Michael & Patricia Fogden/Corbis: 16–17
© Ralph A. Clevenger/Corbis: 5
© Robert and Linda Mitchell: 9, 26
© Stephen Dalton/Photo Researchers, Inc.: 15
© Tim Flach/Getty: cover, 1
© Tom McHugh/Photo Researchers, Inc.: 22

ACKNOWLEDGMENTS
The Child's World®: Mary Berendes, Publishing Director;
Katherine Stevenson, Editor

The Design Lab: Kathleen Petelinsek, Design and Page Production

LIBRARY OF CONGRESS CATALOGING-IN-PUBLICATION DATA
Murray, Peter, 1952 Sept. 29-
 Frogs / by Peter Murray.
    p. cm. — (New naturebooks)
 Includes bibliographical references and index.
 ISBN 1-59296-638-1 (library bound : alk. paper)
 1. Frogs—Juvenile literature. I. Title. II. Series.
 QL668.E2M88 2006
 597.8—dc22   2006001366

Table of Contents

On the cover: A curious red-eyed tree frog peeks out from behind a leaf.

Meet the Frog!

Frogs have been on Earth for about 190 million years.

Frogs live in every area of the world except Antarctica and a few ocean islands. Most frogs can be found in warmer areas of the world where the weather never gets too hot or too cold. They live in trees, on the ground, and in the water. Frogs are almost everywhere!

If you sit quietly by a pond on a warm spring evening, you'll probably hear the chirping of birds. You might also hear the chattering of a nearby squirrel, the quacking of a mother duck, or the splash of a fish jumping. If it's breezy, you'll hear the wind rustling through the leaves and grass. But mostly, you'll hear the peeping, croaking, and bellowing of frogs. The frogs are calling to each other. They are saying, "Here I am! Look at me! Aren't I a fine frog?"

This American bullfrog is hiding among some water plants in a California pond. American bullfrogs grow to be about 5 inches (13 cm) long and can be found all across the United States.

What Do Frogs Sound Like?

In general, large frogs have lower, deeper calls. Small frogs tend to make higher noises that sound more like chirps.

Green tree frogs are sometimes called "cowbell frogs" because their call sounds a little like a cowbell.

Spring is the best time to listen for frogs, but you can hear them all summer long. Most frogs call by filling their **vocal sacs** with air, then forcing the air across their **vocal cords**. Other frogs can make noises without a vocal sac.

Each type of frog has its own call. Tree frogs make a loud trilling, whistling, or peeping sound. Leopard frogs have a snorting, croaking call. Bullfrogs have a deep, booming call that sounds as if they are saying, "Jug-o-rum! Jug-o-rum!"

You can see the big vocal sac of this common reed frog as he sings in Lake Nakuru, Kenya. Common reed frogs have a call that sounds like a tiny bell.

What Are Frogs?

Frogs are different from toads. Frogs have smooth, wet skin, while toads' skin is rough and bumpy. Frogs live both in and out of the water, but toads spend almost all of their lives on land. Frogs have long back legs, while toads' back legs are short and stubby.

A group of frogs is called an *army*.

Like toads and salamanders, frogs are members of an animal group called **amphibians**. Amphibians are cold-blooded—their bodies get warmer or cooler with the temperature of the surrounding air or water. On a hot day, a frog cools itself by staying in the water. On a cool day, it might rest in the sunshine to warm itself.

In colder areas of the world, when winter is coming, frogs burrow into the mud at the bottom of a pond. There they **hibernate**, or go into a deep sleep. The frogs stay buried all winter, waiting for the weather to get warmer. When spring arrives, the frogs dig their way back to the surface.

Waxy monkey tree frogs like this one live in South America. They are called "waxy" because they make a waxy film that they rub on themselves to stay moist. They are called "monkey" frogs because they often walk on all four feet instead of hopping.

Are There Different Kinds of Frogs?

Africa alone has about a thousand different species of frogs.

Some frogs are called "flying frogs" because they can glide from tree to tree. Flying frogs have wider webbing between their toes. When the frogs jump, the webbing catches the air and helps them float through the air.

There are more than 4,700 different types, or **species**, of frogs. The goliath frog from Africa is almost as big as a football and can weigh up to 7 pounds (3 kg)! Some tree frogs, on the other hand, are less than 1 inch (2.5 cm) long.

Depending on where they live, frogs have different kinds of feet. Tree frogs have tiny, sticky pads on their toes that let them cling to smooth leaves or bark. They can even walk on slippery windowpanes! Digging frogs have tiny claws on their back legs to help them scoop dirt and mud. Frogs that spend most of their lives in or near water have webbing between their back toes. The webbing turns their back legs into powerful flippers that help them swim quickly through the water.

This boy is holding a goliath frog. These huge frogs live only in fast-flowing rivers in Cameroon, a nation in western Africa. The frogs' rainforest homes are being destroyed, and people also hunt the frogs for their meat and to sell them as pets. As a result, goliath frogs are becoming very rare.

How Are Baby Frogs Born?

Some frogs can lay up to 4,000 eggs at one time.

Frog eggs are in danger from many things, including hungry fish and even the weather. Only one out of every five eggs will survive to become a frog.

When a female frog is ready to lay her eggs, she answers a male frog's special call. When the male and female find each other, the male climbs onto the female's back. Then he waits for her to lay her eggs in shallow water. As she lays her eggs, the male frog fertilizes them, which causes the eggs to begin developing into baby frogs.

The female lays her eggs in a clump that sticks to plants, grasses, or tree roots in the water. A single clump contains thousands of eggs. Each egg is surrounded by a layer of clear jelly. In just a few days, the eggs hatch.

Top photo: Here you can see common frogs mating in a pond. Their egg clump is right next to them. Common frogs are found in Great Britain.

Bottom photo: From close up, you can see tiny frog babies as they grow inside their clear eggs.

What Are Tadpoles?

Tadpoles are sometimes called *polliwogs*.

One type of poison-dart frog lays its eggs on leaves in the forest. One parent stays with the eggs and waits for them to hatch. When they do, the tadpoles wiggle up onto the parent's back. The adult then carries them to the nearest pond and lets them slip into the water. There, the babies continue to grow.

Like most amphibians, frogs live their lives in two stages. The first stage begins when the eggs hatch. Instead of starting their lives looking like little frogs, the babies come out of the eggs as **tadpoles**. Tadpoles look more like fish than like frogs. They live underwater, feeding on small water plants. Like fish, tadpoles breathe through holes called **gills**. They swim by wiggling their tails back and forth.

Tadpoles have many enemies. Water beetles, fish, birds, and even other frogs like to eat them. Although thousands of tadpoles hatch from one clump of eggs, only a few dozen survive.

14

This common frog tadpole is swimming in a calm pond in Great Britain. It looks nothing like the adult common frogs shown at the top of page 13.

How Do Tadpoles Grow?

Some tadpoles eat other frogs' eggs and even other tadpoles.

A tadpole's arms first appear as little bulges. The bulges get bigger, and the arms finally "pop" out, elbow-first, a few days later.

Tadpoles grow quickly. When a tadpole is old enough, strange things begin to happen. The tadpole's entire body changes! First, two rear legs begin to grow, one on each side of the tail. Then two front legs pop out through the gill holes. The tadpole's mouth gets wider, its eyes get bigger, and its legs get longer and stronger. The gills that allow the tadpole to breathe underwater turn into **lungs**. Now the tadpole can breathe both underwater (through its skin) and above the surface (with its lungs).

Here you can see two red-eyed tree frog tadpoles as they rest in a pond. The larger one has sprouted legs, but it does not yet have its arms. You can see an adult red-eyed tree frog on page 28.

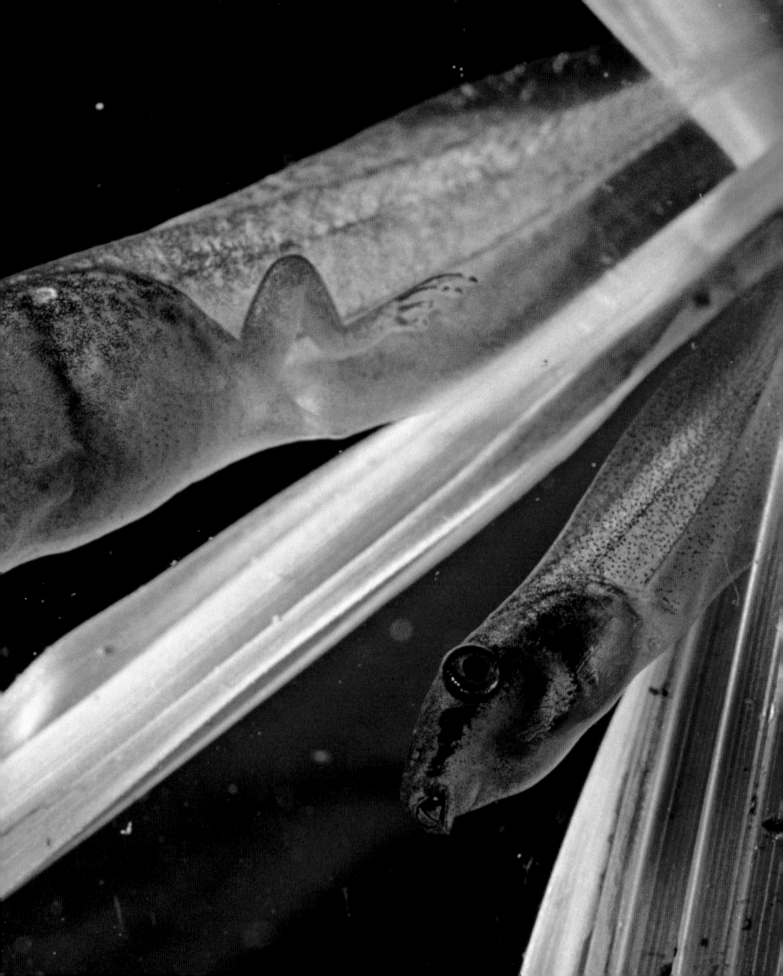

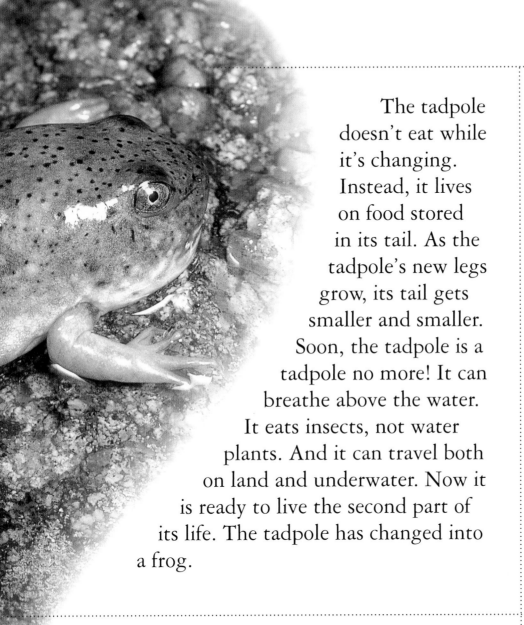

The tadpole doesn't eat while it's changing. Instead, it lives on food stored in its tail. As the tadpole's new legs grow, its tail gets smaller and smaller. Soon, the tadpole is a tadpole no more! It can breathe above the water. It eats insects, not water plants. And it can travel both on land and underwater. Now it is ready to live the second part of its life. The tadpole has changed into a frog.

A very young frog that has just come out of the tadpole stage is often called a *froglet*.

"Amphibian" comes from two Greek words: *amphi* meaning "both," and *bios* which means "life." This refers to the way in which amphibians start their lives in water and later live on land.

This older American bullfrog tadpole is just climbing out of a pond in Pennsylvania. You can see how the tadpole now looks much more like an adult, but it still has its long tadpole tail.

19

What Do Frogs Eat?

Frogs don't drink water—they take it in through their skin.

A frog's bulging eyes allow it to see in all directions.

Frogs have very tiny teeth in the upper parts of their mouths. They don't use their teeth for chewing, however. Instead, they use them for holding onto slippery foods before they swallow them.

After starting its life underwater, a young frog must learn to hunt and eat new kinds of food. Most frogs feed on insects. They might enjoy a big, juicy june bug for lunch and a bunch of flies for an afternoon snack. But how does a frog catch its food, or **prey**? First, the frog sits very still and watches for insects to land or crawl nearby. Suddenly, the frog shoots out its long, sticky tongue. The tongue moves so fast, the prey animal doesn't have time to move out of the way. The tongue quickly brings the prey back to the frog's mouth.

When it swallows, a frog blinks its eyes. Why? Its eyeballs help push the food down its throat! Frogs can eat a lot of insects. In fact, a single frog can eat hundreds of thousands of insects during its lifetime!

20

This frog has just caught a fly with its long, sticky tongue. This picture also shows how frogs must arch their backs and push themselves forward a little to reach faraway bugs.

Some frogs eat more than insects, however. They eat worms, snails, crabs, fish, turtles, and even other frogs. The African bullfrog gobbles mice, rats, birds, and snakes. It sits perfectly still and waits for a small animal to pass by. When one comes close, the frog lunges forward and grabs the prey in its huge mouth. The frog must use its front feet to push large prey animals into its mouth.

African bullfrogs are sometimes called "pixie frogs." This nickname comes from their long scientific name, *Pyxicephalus adsperus*.

In addition to the tiny teeth in the upper parts of their mouths, African bullfrogs have toothlike bumps on their lower jaws. These bumps give the frogs an even better grip on their wiggling foods.

This hungry African bullfrog has caught a rat to eat. African bullfrogs are huge, growing to be about 9 inches (23 cm) long and weighing more than 4 pounds (2 kg). The only frogs that are bigger are goliath frogs.

Do Frogs Have Enemies?

Since its eyes and nose are on top of its body, a frog can see and breathe even while hiding most of its body underwater.

Lots of animals like to eat frogs. Turtles, birds, snakes, large fish, and raccoons all enjoy a frog or two for lunch. In some areas of the world, frogs are eaten by people as well! But frogs have many ways of staying safe. They can dive underwater and hide in the mud for hours at a time. Being slippery and hard to hold also comes in handy. And, of course, frogs can jump. A bullfrog can jump 20 times its own length! If it jumps quickly enough to avoid being eaten, a bullfrog can live for 15 years or more.

This green frog is leaping above the water of its Pennsylvania pond. Its arms help it balance as its powerful hind legs push it upward.

Golden poison-dart frogs are the most poisonous frogs on Earth. They live in the jungles of Colombia, where native people use the frogs' poison on the tips of their hunting darts. Golden poison dart frogs are only about as big as your thumb.

Besides jumping, frogs have another good defense—their coloring. Most frogs have colors and patterns, called **camouflage**, that make them hard to see. Tree frogs are often bright green like leaves, or gray and brown like tree bark. Pond frogs are usually green or dull brown, so they blend in with the pond's plants and mud.

Poison-dart frogs stay safe in another way— their bodies make a poison that comes out through their skin. All poison-dart frogs have bright colors that warn enemies to stay away.

Can you find the two Malayan horned frogs in this picture? They are camouflaged to look just like the leaves of the Malaysian forest floor where they live.

Although frogs have many enemies, their greatest threat comes from people. Every year, we drain the water from thousands of ponds, swamps, and marshes. We dump millions of gallons of pollutants and garbage into rivers and streams. Using their camouflage, jumping far, and diving deep can't help the frogs when their **habitat** is destroyed.

We can help frogs survive by preserving our wetlands and keeping our rivers, lakes, and ponds clean. If we all do our part, everyone can hear the peeping, croaking, and bellowing of frogs for thousands of years to come.

"Jug-o-rum! Jug-o-rum!"

Since frogs take in air and water through their skin, sick frogs often mean that the air or water is unhealthy for people, too! Scientists now watch frogs closely, especially in city areas. If they find sick frogs, they do studies to be sure that the air and water are safe and clean—for both people and frogs.

This red-eyed tree frog is clinging to a leaf. These frogs (also called leaf frogs) live throughout Central America and are active at night. It's thought that their red eyes frighten animals that might try to eat them.

Glossary

amphibians (am-FIB-ee-yenz) Amphibians are cold-blooded animals that live their lives in two stages (in the water as babies and on land as adults). Frogs are amphibians.

camouflage (KAM-oo-flazh) Camouflage is coloring that helps an animal hide or blend in with its surroundings. Most frogs have camouflage that looks like the plants, water, or mud around them.

gills (GILZ) Gills are organs on the sides of fish and young amphibians that allow them to breathe underwater.

habitat (HAB-ih-tat) An animal's habitat is the type of environment in which it lives. Frogs habitats range from marshes and wetlands to drier areas.

hibernate (HYB-er-nayt) When an animal hibernates, it does into a very deep sleep. Frogs hibernate during cold winter months by burrowing into the mud.

lungs (LUNGZ) Lungs are organs that allow animals and people to breathe air. Adult frogs have lungs.

prey (PREY) Animals that are hunted and eaten by other animals are prey. Insects, worms, and fish are common prey for frogs.

species (SPEE-sheez) A species is a different type of an animal. There are over 4,700 different species of frogs.

tadpoles (TAD-pohlz) Tadpoles are baby frogs or toads. Tadpoles live underwater and look more like little fish than frogs or toads.

vocal cords (VOHK-ull KORDZ) Vocal cords are bands in the throats of people and animals. When air passes over these bands, they move and produce sounds.

vocal sacs (VOHK-ull SAKS) A frog's vocal sac is a pouch below its mouth. When the frog calls, it fills the sac with air, and then pushes the air across its vocal cords.

To Find Out More

Read It!

Arnosky, Jim. *All About Frogs.* New York: Scholastic, 2002.

French, Vivian, and Alison Bartlett (illustrator). *Growing Frogs.* Cambridge, MA: Candlewick Press, 2000.

Lacey, Elizabeth, and Christopher Santoro (illustrator). *The Complete Frog: A Guide for the Very Young Naturalist.* New York: Lothrop, Lee & Shepard Books, 1989.

Souza, D. M. *Frogs, Frogs Everywhere.* Minneapolis, MN: Carolrhoda, 1995.

Vern, Alex. *Where Do Frogs Come From?* San Diego: Harcourt, 2001.

Winer, Yvonne, and Tony Oliver (illustrator). *Frogs Sing Songs.* Watertown, MA: Charlesbridge, 2003.

On the Web

Visit our home page for lots of links about frogs:
http://www.childsworld.com/links

Note to Parents, Teachers, and Librarians: We routinely check our Web links to make sure they're safe, active sites—so encourage your readers to check them out!

31

Index

About the Author

Peter Murray has written more than a hundred children's books on science, nature, history, and other topics. An animal lover, Pete lives in Golden Valley, Minnesota, in a house with one woman, two poodles, several dozen spiders, thousands of microscopic dust mites, and an occasional mouse.